This is an heroic narrative poem centering around one of the greatest events in history, the coming of the Iron Age. The story opens in Ireland of the Bronze Age and passes into Gaul where the Iron Age is developing. The period is soon after the taking of Rome by the Gauls (300 B.C.) when the Celts are making themselves the dominant people in Western Europe. With the theme of change, which means the rise of violence and the passing of an ancient order, there goes a romantic story. A boy sees his father murdered by his uncle and dreams of using the warriors he has heard of, the iron-armed Gauls, against his father's slayers and establishing the new kind of kingship, the kingship based on power and not on

(Continued on back flap)

situations are dramatic—sometimes striking fire in wrath, sometimes touched with a dreamy tenderness. The peculiar richness of the Celtic imagination makes the scenes vivid; the characters speak with the Irish gift for phrase, and the poem moves in the rich light of legendary things passionately remembered and given an authentic reality.

The illustrations in black and white by the young Irish artist, Séan O'Sullivan, vividly convey the spirit of the age.

THE STORY OF LOWRY MAEN

Books by PADRAIC COLUM

Poems

The Legend of St. Columba

The Big Tree of Bunlahy

The Road Round Ireland

Cross Roads in Ireland

The Story of Lowry Maen

By

PADRAIC COLUM

NEW YORK

THE MACMILLAN COMPANY

1937

TO

THE MEMORY OF

MICHAEL COLLINS

PREFACE

THERE is a passage in one of Matthew Arnold's poems which, when we think of times before the beginning of West European history, supplies the generality of us with human associates. There is the "grave Tyrian trader," who, one sunrise, descries an emerging prow, a Greek coaster's, and knows "the intruders on his ancient home, The young light-hearted Masters of the Waves," and who thereupon sails out into the Atlantic, to where "down cloudy cliffs, through sheets of foam," his new clients come. They are "shy traffickers, the dark Iberians." It is altogether a superb piece of picture-making in verse. And the figures of the supplanted Tyrian who "on the beach undid his corded bales," the forward-coming Greek, the remotely-dwelling Iberian who has to be initiated into the ways of commerce, personalize for us when we try to envisage it, the Age of Bronze in Western Europe.

But the West European of the Bronze Age was not so unused to trafficking as the poet of the Scholar Gypsy would have us believe. In Tartassos the Iberians themselves had a centre of commerce and culture that was the western counterpart of the Tyrian trader's home-port. The Atlantic routes were known to the Tartassians. Ireland, a gold-producing country at the time, was their link with the Baltic, with Britain and Brittany. And in the three Atlantic countries, Brittany, Britain and Ireland, there were long-established social orders as we can see from the solemn piles of Carnac and Stonehenge and the less impressive grave-mounds by the Boyne. The gold-work of Ireland remains to show us that Western Europe was producing objects that could be prized in Eastern Mediterranean centres.

However, the narrative that this is a preface to is not a survey of the people of the Bronze Age and their activities. That they had a settled order and a culture of some complexity is all I wish to maintain. The theme of the narrative is the break-up of an ancient order and the coming of a new order. The order that is broken up is that of the Bronze Age in Ireland; the order that takes its place is that of the Iron Age.

I take it for granted that the people of the Bronze Age in Ireland were not different from the people of the historical period, that the main part of them were a Celtic people living according to Celtic customs.[1]

People are apt to put at the beginning of their history a long period of unwarlike stability with some long-lived King as its representative and patron—the age of Osiris in Egypt, of Numa in Italy. This period of stability is broken up by family violence, a new order is tragically inaugurated, and with an age of unconscious unity behind them the people have to find their way to an age of conscious unity. In Irish tradition the King who represents the long-enduring stability was named Ugony More: he was just before the last King of the Bronze Age. His great-grandson, Lowry Loingsech, Lowry the Voyager, to avenge the murder of his father and to reclaim the kingship, brought into Ireland the iron-armed warriors from Gaul and so inaugurated the Iron Age. The story is historical but with a legendary pattern.

[1] According to the French Celticist, Henri Hubert. The Gaels, he argues, were the first wave of the Celtic expansion; they settled in Ireland at the very beginning of the Bronze Age, coming there by ship from their homeland by the North Sea. The Gauls or Brythons were the second wave of the expansion, coming south and west from Central Europe.

But can we think of the Bronze Age as giving a long period of unwarlike stability and have we justification for believing that the iron-armed men inaugurated an age that was relatively more violent? I do not know. I remember that the men whose violence Homer glorified and Hesiod deplored used bronze (but it should be noted that they were a baronage in a country in which they were not quite settled) and that the terrifying fort, Dun Aonghusa on Arran, is there to show us that men of the Bronze Age had to make a mighty effort to defend themselves. Yet because iron can be more destructive than bronze we can well believe that the users of the long iron swords were more dedicated to battle than the users of bronze. And we can believe that the Iron Age tended towards a militarily organized kingship, a more secular one, than the Age of Bronze: the new sanctions would be those of force while the old ones would have been religious. The peacefulness of the Bronze Age as reflected in the figure of Ugony More may be only a myth, but it is a myth that gives significance to his great-grandson's designs and deeds.

The Iron Age was inaugurated much later in Ireland than on the Continent. The Gauls came into Ireland after the taking of Rome—about 300 B.C. It was the period of Celtic expansion on the Continent when "Celtic tribes, with their great broad-swords, their war-chariots and champion fighting, swept over Central and Western Europe, everywhere making themselves masters of the earlier population, and planting their great entrenched forts on every hilltop from Ireland to Bohemia." [1] At the time of this narrative Gaul was being rapidly Celticised: the Celtic tribes were spreading south; they had made contact with the Greeks who a century before had founded Marseilles. And Celtic bands had reached the old centre of Western culture and commerce, Tartassos. The Greeks knew of a King of Tartassos famous for his riches and liberality: his name was Argonthonios; it is Celtic, containing the word for silver. The name of a Celtic leader who threatened Marseilles has been recorded and I have used it as the name of the overking whom Lowry Maen served—Catumandus. Like many of the Celtic names in inscriptions on the Continent or recorded by Greek or Roman historians it is properly a title: He-who-directs-the-Battle. And this is the place to note that "Brennus" was not a personal name:

[1] Christopher Dawson: "The Age of the Gods".

[xi]

the army that captured Rome fought under the auspices of the War God who in Ireland was Bran or Brian; this army would have been known to the Celtic world as The Followers of Bran.

The presence of gold, the fact that the country lay across the route to the Baltic where that most precious of all substances, amber, was obtained, and that the early trade-route to Britain and Brittany was through it, made Ireland an important centre in the "Age of the Gods" that was before the "Age of the Heroes," and long before the "Age of Men." There were fairs then to which merchants came. But games as in ancient Greece, assemblies for the promulgation of judgments were primary at these fairs. They had their origin in the funeral games which were kept up for some divinized ancestor. Undoubtedly a recital of the deeds of the one in whose honor the fair was held, or of some active descendant of his, or of some notable contemporary was part of what went on. The story of the hero of this narrative would surely have been related at the fair which for over a thousand years was held in the territory he belonged to. I imply that it was. A story-teller who is on his way to take part in the recitals, rehearses, I would have readers suppose, this story in some magnate's house.

It is, in my own mind, part of a sequence which may get written. The epical material in Irish tradition has been exploited by modern poets, but the sagas of various historical personages have not been worked over. It might be practicable to put some of these sagas into a sequence—the ones that have the possibility of swiftly moving narrative—and so accomplish a rough kind of "Shah-Nemeh." The second in the imagined sequence would deal with the sixth-century attempt to bring the North into an Irish polity, and would be entitled "The Lays of King Downal and Prince Congal Claen."

THE FIRST PART

"No youngster ever had so much to tell
Of all he sees when he is journey-bound,"
Said Croftnie the Harp-player to the lad,
As following Prince Leary's in their own
Chariot they sped.

"Croftnie, now I see
The twisting spokes and bronze rims of the wheels
That bear my father's chariot, and I see
The springing deer, the rising flocks of birds.
The men who guard the fords that we splash through
And guard the causeways have curved blades of
    bronze
On lengthy handles and wear leathern cloaks.
And now the forest with its heavy branches
And gorges where the rocks are shaped like dragons,
Where shouting boys are driving grunting swine.
The forest of itself makes other sound—
What is it, Croftnie, you that listen well?"

"The sound the acorns make in falling down—
A galloping sound."

"What see you, Croftnie?"
[3]

"The change, I think, that's coming over all.
Your father's grandfather, Ugony the Great,
Had set a mould of custom round men's ways:
He lived so long that he
Had broken Change to be a household beast—
The wild-lynx Change went softly through the land:
Music greatly flourished
Since there were no debates to din it down,
No wars to clash it from the people's ears.
But long-lived Ugony the Great is dead:
Now Change will growl and snarl and tear flesh—
I see her widely opened wild-lynx eyes."

"But now my father goes to take the rule."

"He is a worthy Prince, none worthier
To set his feet upon the Stone of Kings,
But wide as to the Northern Islands where
The sky-larks sing all night, the gap between
His time and Ugony's, if I know aught."

Where sky-larks sing all night—was that as far
As where the ship had come from? the lad asked,
Mentioning the ship that had come in from Gaul.

[4]

Its traffickers would come up to the fair
That was in memory of Tighernmas
Who back in ancient times first smelted gold,
And thereby gave us means to pay for metal,
And stuffs and wares, and have besides the craft
Of shaping gold: all this the Harper told him
As the chariots turned towards the fair.
Prince Leary would keep ancient custom up,
And figure at the fair before he went
To set his feet upon the Stone of Kings.

The beach was reached; above it was the green
Where the fair was, the games and the assembly—
The ship was to be seen.

                     That ship from Gaul!
It was not spoken of by Leary's son—
It was too strange to wonder at, too lone:
It sank into his memory as sinks
Into the water's depth an offering
Made to the guardian of an uncrossed lake.

Amber and jet the traffickers had brought
Up from the ship with other stuffs and wares,

[5]

And set their jet and amber by our bronze—
Trumpets and level swords; the ribs of gold
That are our riches were well eyed by them,
And the wrought gold which cerds of ours who have
Chief supply have customed skill in shaping:
There were the thin gold crescents, and besides
A sunlike piece, ribbed, ridged, and whorled
That would be the chief treasure of a King
Whose realm was beyond Dunuvius River.

Croftnie made mention of the things of note
To Leary's son. "Amber," he said, "is here—
These wedge-like pieces on a deer-skin laid:
Burnished by sunshine in a northern land,
The autumn leaves have color like these pieces."
"Now one speaks with my father," said the lad,
"And I would listen to his strange-toned speech."
"He is the chief of merchants," Croftnie said.

"Iron is harder, and with iron, swords
Can be made longer by another reach,"
And these words answered Leary who had asked
How lengthier swords and harder could be made,
Seeing the merchant turn from the bronze.

[6]

"In Gaul and in Beyond-Gaul men have forged
Iron into swords, and with such weapons
New lands, rich treasures gain in east and south.
A leader of the Gauls
Got gold to weigh his sword and scabbard down
When a head-city, Rome,
Was taken by the Followers of Bran."

"What makes he on the ground?" asked Leary's son.

"The Sign of Bran," said Croftnie, and the lad,
"I'll look upon the Sign." But Croftnie said,
"The War-god Bran—back with him into Gaul,"
For he knew tribes that kept the name of Bran
Living upon the fringes of the realm
Ugony had ruled—great Ugony who was dead.

But now a man upon a coppery horse
Rode up beside the chariots and the guards.
"My father's name he shouts," said Leary's son.

"The news he's brought sends us another way,"
Said Croftnie, "we go through Cavach's lands,
Cavach, your father's brother who is dead

[7]

As told the messenger. The kin would have your
    father
Stand with the mourners by Prince Cavach's bier."

"The twisting spokes and bronze rims of the wheels
That bear my father's chariot I see,
With guards beside it running with their spears
Held lengthwise and their cloaks of otter-skin.
What see you, Croftnie, in this open land?"

"The Gaul your father spoke with talked of iron
In use beyond the sea. A prophecy
May be fulfilled: it is that when men use
A dark, dense metal Change will surely come."

"But that is far away. Will what I look on
Be different? Look, Croftnie—
Geese gather in a hollow and smoke rises
Through roofs of wattled houses; sparks are blowing
Out of a cerd's house, and a woman's milling
Her grain in a stone's hollow with a stone—
Croftnie, will these things change?"

    "I do not know:
But long-lived Ugony the Great is dead:

[8]

Here are Prince Cavach's cattle with their herdsman;
I know the mark that's on them. There's the mound:
And there's Prince Cavach's house upon the mound.
Your uncle will not take you on his knee."

"Croftnie, I know. He will not, being dead."

"And will be buried in the ancient way
As told the messenger—you will see it so.
Cavach, the crafty brother, is no more.
He might have edged a place too close to him
Who'll set his feet upon the Stone of Kings."

Below the mound on which was Cavach's house
An unyoked chariot was placed for burial.
The man upon the coppery horse dismounted,
And bent his knee to what was in the chariot,
A stiff and swathed figure, and went away,
Drawing the guards who were with Leary's chariot.

Lifting his head to sniff to where they came,
Leaping the shafts, rubbing against the wheels,
A tame wolf ranged; beside the chariot
No people stood, and Leary's son looked on

[9]

Only the creature in which tameness strove
With wildness: then he saw his father cross
The sward and stand near where the wood-dog
    strained.

The figure that was stiff upon the chariot
Raised itself, a spear was in those hands.
And the lad saw the figure thrust the spear:
His father fell
First on his knee, and then the figure, standing
Upon the chariot, drove the spear down through him.
The body lay
Like a cut tree; the spear-wielder sprang down.

He heard a whisper:
"Leary is dead; Cavach, his brother killed him;
They've cut our guards off from us; we'll not live."
And then he ran to where his father lay,
And thence was dragged to face a dark-faced man
Who stood beneath a tree with men about him,
His followers who held long, ready spears.

And he was helpless there—not even the words
He formed to fling into that face would come;

Only his breath he heard; he knew he'd lost
The use of speech; he formed the words again:
"Maen," "Speechless" was the word they used of him.
"Your father's in the burial-chariot now;
I'll be the one to follow the old King,
And turn the Kingship into mine own line."
The lad would speak; he tried once more and could
    not,
And heard himself named "Maen" by those about.

Then Cavach said, "There is no need to slay
A speechless one. Never can he dispute
The Kingship with me nor those born of me."
"You'll let Maen live?" asked Harper Croftnie.
"I'll let him live," said Cavach, "take him hence—
Not to his father's, for that house goes down,
But where you will." Then Croftnie took him up
And carried him; he held a body stiffened
Against his own, and went forsaken paths.

   They went far that day
And reached a mark famous for sight and sound—
A waterfall with a cromlech nigh it:
There Croftnie the Harper set him down—

The lad who had no name but what was flung him—
Under the cromlech of a King whose name
Was lost before great Ugony's was heard of.
And the rain washed from the stones and streamed
To where the river swelled; the trees were black,
And there was nothing for a man to look at
In all the land but the wide face of the rain.

THE SECOND PART

Not in Prince Leary's chariot, but on foot
The two went now, unanswering helpmates,
And, as men will who'd have their ways unfound,
They lengthened out their journey: on a day
They came where trees were sunken; Croftnie spied
Elks' horns lying wide upon the ground,
And said, "We are forgotten as these horns,"
And then they went towards where a river gleamed.

And he said too, "The one who'll refuge us
Is my own fosterer, an old, old man
Who looks into deep pools and whose own mind
Is deep enough to hold the stories told
Of men who lived before MacCeacht, MacGrian,
MacDaire held the land, and on the pool
Of that deep mind the story we will tell
Will stay like new-pulled grass." To him they went,
With him they stayed; young Maen there grew tall.

Then one day Croftnie looking towards the flats
Saw the islet where the swans had nested,
And saw the cygnets; they were full-grown now,
And one stood on a ridge and stretched his wings.
Proudly he stretched them: inside they were
Pure white—the livery of a swan was there.
Then Croftnie knew how many times he'd watched
The cygnets change and proudly show their change.
Now the short passage, fifty years to sixty,
Was made for him, and for his fosterling
The long passage, eight years to its teen.

How lived they while one withered and one grew?
The old, old man had craft of weaving boats
For river-fishers—they were rounds of rods
Covered with hide—and had craft of knitting
Nets that could take the wariest of prey.
There Maen who was all patiences learned these
    crafts,
Fished in the river and was ferry-man
For those who'd cross, and living with these two—
His fosterer and that deep-eyed old man
Whose life went back to the old God of the Waters,
To Nuada Neacht who had taught his crafts,

He grew to be a stripling, and was one
Most daring: he was bold enough to turn
Upon the wolves that one time followed them—
Turn upon them without the hunter's shout,
Being worldless always—never else than "maen,"
Though Croftnie would dream that he could hear him
Show him as only words of man can show
The stuff was in his mind and all he hoped for,
But never that, and he would see him make
Upon the ground the sign that was Bran's sign.

When the swans flew, Croftnie told the lad,
They would be done with this craft by the river.
Maen looked upon the cygnets wide of wing,
But muddy colored by their sires and dams,
And looked upon the crossed and pointed rods
Whose ends were stuck into the ground, and signed
That he would make another woven boat.
He stood straight up, covered with otter-skins,
A lean, tall youth, and with a wedge-shaped face
Narrow below and broad at temple-hollows,
And with a bulge of amber-colored hair
Over grey, open eyes—eyes that were bright
As shining metal or as shining water,

And were as steady as the eyes that look out
On far and lonely things; his mouth was shut,
And looked as if a hand when it was soft
Had closed it. Yet was the lad alert:
The wild duck warying her swimming brood
He heard, and he could follow in the half-light
The small chicks with the hurrying water-hen. . . .

O Story-teller, since the fire went low
We have not seen your eyes nor seen your face!

I lie upon the bench; my eyes are closed.

Will you not bring us forward in the tale?

My listeners know why I should have fresh mind
Before I bring young Maen and Croftnie
To place of refuge from beside the river.

But still the night is young; we would hear you.

Then backward in my tale: the cromlech where
With Croftnie's cloak around him Maen lay
On wet fern underneath the topping-stone,

[18]

And shook with fever when he stood upright.
Backward to the morning after dumbness
Had stricken the young lad; when they first knew
Themselves for waifs, the waif's day before them.

Women and children carrying their pots
And pails and churns, with the herders going
And cattle headed for the mountain-pasture,
Came on the pair and let them fare along.
And they who'd looked upon a King's death came
To sleep in bothies built of sods and feel
The wind blow through the sods, to sup on curds,
And have for meat the hedgehog baked in clay,
Or young crows luckily caught before their use
Of wings, and small birds taken with a flare.

Maen's fever went, but words did not come back,
And often Croftnie came upon the lad
Perched on a rock and watching down below,
Or questing, questing like a hawk that's mazed.

And when the herdsmen broke the booley up,
They left the mountain by the other slope,
And so to Croftnie's fosterer's . . . that's past.

Unto the cromlech they have come again.
Croftnie bids his fosterling remember
The darkened day that brought them here before.
The stripling looks upon the ancient stones
As long as I look through the chimney-hole
On that red-fired star that rides these nights.

THE THIRD PART

Unto the one whose pillar-stone's outside
The Harper brought young Maen, and his house
Was as this house is, goodly in all ways.
He had but little doubt, the House-master,
That he whom Croftnie brought was Leary's son,
But asked no certainties upon that score.

The youths about the house—
The fosterlings of that protecting lord,
Soon ceased to feel
An oddness in the name that meant such lack,
For he was not a heavy-going lad
As the dumb are, but had a noted quickness,
And he was liked because he'd guard the others,
Seeing each got his meed of praise and boon:
He came to be a leader in their sports,
And was the one they talked about, as though
Guessing a ruling manhood in the lad,
As boys will in the one of master-ways.
But Maen was "maen," one who could never rule.

Now green stalks raised themselves above the grass,
Holding up pods of gold, and they were broom,
And golden blossoms spread upon the furze,

[23]

And all the sounds were pleasant as on ship
When every strain and creak
Tell how the air and water have grown kind,
And skies propitious. Croftnie tuned his harp;
It was to play unto a band of youths
Under an ash-tree that had budded branches,
And had a storm-cock singing in its top.

So they fared to face the fosterlings
Of another house, and play the hurley-game.
Loud-mouthed, prancing lads, each one striving
To be to the fore whether in words or movement,
Their troop went through the golden-blossomed
    furze,
Maen leading, Croftnie coming after them.
The Harper looking on their rank was heartened,
And had pride in them, in their venturesomeness,
And took pride in the youths who waited them,
Each with his hurley-stick upon his shoulder
With yellow meadow-flowers twining it,
And made his harp sound for those stripling-bands
As though they were the tops and props of men.
They marched around the playing-field sunwise,
And then began the game; Croftnie rejoiced

In that unstinted energy of theirs—
The rush, the speed, the sweep, the cunning stroke.

Two lads stood out from the opposing sides,
And one was Maen; the other was a lad
Who was so bent on winning that he made
His game a war and every stroke a battle,
And all he did was countered cunningly
By Maen; then a hawk swooped on the ball,
Caught it and dropped it; where it fell, the two
Together were: the ball was in a hollow:
As knee to knee they strove, the others stood
Ready to pitch themselves upon the ball.
Suddenly a stroke
Broke Maen's hurling-stick across; he stood,
And the two faced each other in the field.
A dark-faced one Maen saw with lips that bared
His teeth; he knew that face. "King Cavach's son!"
He cried. "The son of him
Who slew my father—never royal man,
But one who wrongfully took a King's place!"

Then all the lads were startled into shouting
"The Speechless speaks!" "Lowry Maen!" they cried,

[25]

And gathered round to look upon the lad
On whom words came with suddenness of fire
Bursting through thatch—"Lowry Maen!" they cried.
Only the dark-faced one, King Cavach's son,
Remained apart, leaning on his hurley.
Then Croftnie knew that there had come to pass
A desperate turn; the very name they raised
Spoke present danger; spears would soon surround
Prince Leary's son and Ugony's great-grandson,
One who could speak as well as any King!

He struck the harp-strings, and the Laughter Tune
He played; they laughed around him, the lads all—
Even Cavach's son turned a smiling face,
And Lowry Maen, to where one pointed
A shape that made them happy, for all saw
In every weed, in every bush, such shape
As Croftnie played upon the bright harp-strings.

Leaving the lads in laughter at a bush
That looked, because a sapling grew beside it,
Like an old man leaning upon his stick,
The Harper drew away Prince Leary's son.
"Again we have to go as castaways,
And hide in deeper burrows than before;

Our lives were but half-hidden then, but now
They'll need to be whole-hidden. Whither now?
I'll have to stir more quickly than my wont
Has been these times back." Then to him his charge:
"I will to Gaul. Bring me to where the ship
Comes. The cerds were making all things ready
For call of merchants making harbour where
King Cavach's messenger came on my father.
Take me to that ship-stead. Before Cavach's
Searchers can find me, I'll be on that ship."

  In two days' time
The Harper and his fosterling were there,
Their gaze upon the ship that was a piece
Of a strange world. "Be sure that I'll be back
With warriors armed with iron weapons
To break King Cavach's rule and re-establish
The line of Ugony in my father's son."
This Lowry Maen, looking the young King, said.
"And I shall triumph with you," he was told,
"And yet shall rue the day your triumph comes,
For it will be a day will surely make
What's foreign, ours, as it will what's native
Like tangled wool cast in the discard-heap."

[27]

"But you have something else to say to me,"
Said Lowry Maen, and said his fosterer,
"Such must be; and you whom change has chosen,
Must go and come from lands where there are powers
Guessed at by us here; go, then, where conquest
Is in men's thoughts, where Kings' words are com-
     mands
To soldiers who will gather realms to them.
Go there, and I shall see before I die
Your rule established over Ugony's land."

But not yet could he go towards that new life:
He had yet to mingle
Blood from his veins with blood of other men
Who would adopt him into brotherhood,
And that would be under the ancient oak
Upon whose bark were many Gaulish signs.
And now one called him to the ship; he went
Into a curragh, bidding Croftnie wait.

THE FOURTH PART

He who was King Cavach's son,
Conaing, came where two youths were waiting,
Bringing another, and the four then went
Dinning each other with their talk and boasts.
"Seoriah's," the word was, "To King Seoriah's."

And at that morning-hour
King Seoriah upon his lawn stepped out,
His wife and daughter with him, and behold!
There was a file of claimants on the lawn.
"What do they here?" said Seoriah, and his wife:
"Their sheep have cropped my household-stuff, the
    woad
That the vat waited, and my steward marked
The faulting flock: 'Tis this that brings them here:
To scrape a judgment off you, King Seoriah."

Seoriah looked upon the file of men:
Long-faced, lanky; mountainy men they were;
Great arguers; they'd stand from dawn to dark,
And wear a King out of his sense of right.
" 'Tis not my day for judgment," Seoriah said,
And left them standing there, and with his wife
And virgin-daughter, Miria
Went where the sun warmed stones; they sat them
    down
And looked upon a lake.

Seoriah's wife
Had basket of soft feathers she had plucked
From necks and breasts of her own geese that were

The whitest and the softest-feathered flock
The country had. She and Miria now
Filled bolster-covers, while King Seoriah
Wearing his coat of well-woven horses' hair,
The pick of Kings of all small realms appeared.

    "The fault's in me,
Or rather in my people," said his wife,
"For you, King Seoriah,
Are but an awkward and plain-visaged man:
King Ugony used to say:
'My sons and grandsons—would that they had mar-
    ried
With those fine people; I'd have handsome heads
And shapely bodies to keep up my name'—
I only tell you what King Ugony said,
For everything he said should be remembered."

This talk's beginning was the house-daughter
Whose breasts had depth now beneath her bodice.
"What will you do with me?" Miria said.

So she would speak and so turn to a youth,
Her mother thought—"What will you do with me?"
"Your father will stay with you all the day,

And I will be beside you in the night,
And this must be until a choice is made
Amongst the youths who'd take you to his house:
Each is so jealous of the other now—
Conaing, Naale, Sedna and Aleel—
That each would try to kill the one you favor,
And we would have to pay for the blood shed
About our precinct, and not small the price
If it should fall out that a prince's son
Had life struck out of him about this place—
We'll have to see you give no special glances."
Miria laughed. "I will give none, my mother,"
And looked across the lake, and told herself
The month that brings
Milk to the ewes, Oimilc, now was here
With pleasantness of feasting and of games,
And one she favored might stand close to her
During some merriment, nor be forbid.

And now King Seoriah welcomed on his lawn
Conaing and Naale, Sedna and Aleel,
While with her fine bone needle, Miria
Stitched, her head bent, and her careful mother,
Who had a reckoning eye, glanced at the youths.

     Conaing and Naale:
They had been reared in Cavach's house together,
And were of equal age, but those who gave
Commands to weaponed men, put Naale
Before, and far before, King Cavach's son.
     He was big-bodied,
Had bold address, and could with sureness judge
An issue, and was ready with his blade,
While Cavach's son with his high, narrow head,
And watching eyes, and waiting ways, and sudden
Silent approach, was like a King's steward
More than a King's heir. Sedna and Aleel—
They were as good as any two youths going,
And never would be blamed or greatly named.

Now as Seoriah led them to his door,
Men stood out and asked him for his judgment.
" 'Tis not my day for judging," said Seoriah.
"I'll leave it to this young man," he said then,
"A King's son, he can give a judgment here.
Conaing judges who is Cavach's son."
"The sheep whose cropping left the Queen without
Her woad, go to the Queen: impound them then
Until her shepherd takes them to her field."

But the men cried, "This hits no judgment—
He's no King's son who gives such judgments."
" 'Tis not my day for judging," said Seoriah.
And brought the four guests through his open door.

King Seoriah's House of Welcomes—it was famous!
Thick-walled, thick-thatched, and with an un-
    quenched fire
Upon its hearth, it had held companies
Around its board or on its benches since
Times ago when Ugony's reign began,
And no one had gone out through its wide door
Without the wish of joining once again
With those who talked around its board or hearth.

A salmon that King Seoriah's fisherman
Brought in with pride was broiled upon the coals,
And made a feast; meal-cakes with butter topped
And water-cress went likewise on the board.
And when the feast was finished an old man
Who kept his corner since his hands were palsied,
Told of King Ugony, that royal man
Whom he had played before, being a Harper.
And since there was no harp-playing for this time,

Aleel and Sedna, who had pleasant voices,
Sang, first one and then the other,
Old songs King Seoriah called for from his couch:
From Gorias, from Falias, they came
Or Findrias or Murias, these songs,
And they were better liked than are the songs
We have now, for even songs decline,
And none we hear to-day are half as good
As the old songs that pleased King Ugony.

Her mother thought Miria's gaze too long
Stayed upon Sedna, and she had the girl
Bring each of the four youths the honey-drink.
And then 'twas bed-time; Miria went
Behind the leathern curtain with her mother,
And Seoriah and his guests lay on the couches.
Miria's turning made her mother say,
"The quietness I'll have when you will lie
Beside another—I will welcome it!"

Listening for Sedna's voice Miria heard
Her father speak, "We'll all go to the Fair,
The four of you, and I—Miria, too
For she can ride behind me on the pilion.

[37]

We will all go—there will be wine from Gaul,
And it is long since I had taste of wine."
She wondered would she see the ship from Gaul—
A ship would be more strange than tower or cloud,
And it brought someone somewhere. Then she heard
The old man moving to the door: he spoke
Of something in his memory, for he muttered,
"It hits no judgment: he is no King's son."

Their way was down through rough defiles and passes
Where hollies grew and pale-leaved mountain-ashes,
And at high noon the six of them were walking
Among the sights and sounds of that thronged Fair.

And with the throng the six went to the Green
Where sports were held: it was between two markets,
The Foreigners' Market and the Food Market,
And as they went they glimpsed all sorts of men
From royalties to horse-boys. Lads led hounds:
All trust and expectation went the hounds:
They looked as if they knew
Another minute would bring them on the trail
That led to the boar's wallow or stag's lair.

The chief event, the crowning sport was on:
A new-come horse, a Gaulish horse, brought over
Upon the ship, was given the course to race on.
Upon its hoofs, plain to be seen, were irons
That gleamed as sods of turf were cast from them,
And fire was struck from flints. What kind of men
Where there beyond the seas whose horses' hoofs
Were shod so—shod with iron?
The throng stood wondering at the galloper!

Horn-blowers, tumblers, pipers, story-tellers
Kept up such revel that a man could stay
From dawn to dark to watch and listen to them:
But now Seoriah, tired of being an onlooker,
Or with a throat that claimed the wine of Gaul,
Left the Green, Miria at his side.
He told the young men he should look for them
In the Market of the Foreigners.

Fires were glimmering on the Cooking-slope.
Aleel and Sedna who had little ease
Beside the other pair—as little as
The small hawks have beside the hawks of bulk—
Felt appetite and went up from the Green.

[39]

Caldrons were seething over fires, spits turning,
Meal-cakes were baking upon heated stones.
Aleel and Sedna going here and there,
Ate small birds taken off the spits, with cakes
In honey dipped, and listened to the stories
Told of the ones in whose remembrance
The Fair was held and the Fair days kept sacred.

Conaing with Naale watched the second race:
Now, as King Cavach's son spied on the crowd
He saw a gillie carrying a harp.
Seeing the harp with a swan's head on it
Carved, Conaing knew
The Harp-player was not away, and where
Croftnie was, there Lowry Maen would be.

That rash reviler—
Leary's son and Ugony's great-grandson:
He'd have his father's spearmen meet him here,
And that coil would be ended easily.
Telling his comrade he would not return
With them, nor be a guest at Seoriah's,
He went to where his horse was and rode off.
His father was where chariots were being builded,
And that was near at hand: he would go there.

That Cavach's son would not be guest with them
Was not rued greatly by big-bodied Naale,
For he himself yearned for Miria.
He had not slept all night for thinking on
Seoriah's daughter; his passion with the moon
Had grown, and now
The thought of her mastered his every thought,
And she, he knew, would sooner go to him
Than to Conaing, or either of the others.
Upon the road or in the house she might
Be drawn to him and give him glance or clasp,
And 'twould be well that there would not be three,
But two to deal with; his hand clenched, and he
Handled his blade, seeing the two young men
Aleel and Sedna, coming up to him.
Then turning from where men with headless spears
Fought up and down, he went to where were blades
For buyers, and he changed
The blade he carried for a better blade,
And went to find Seoriah and his daughter.

The traffickers who saw her from their booths
Knew that they would carry
In their minds a measure of rare beauty—

[41]

A face and form that were like the gold
Rings that were the measure of true value.
Her father bought her weighty bracelets
Of bronze; then he would have her look on
The ship that had found track to their far land.

Seoriah his beakers full had taken,
And it had pleasured the young maid to look on
The lines of ordered booths, bright stuffs and wares,
And now they went out to the water-side.
She saw the ship and looked with wonder on it,
And Seoriah found beside the oak whose branches
Were the last living thing the land put forth,
A Harper: more than for wine of Gaul
He had a longing now to hear fine music.
The Harper played and with a master-hand
As Seoriah found out when he asked the boon.

THE FIFTH PART

And Lowry Maen
Back from the Gaulish ship, looked on the hills
That rimmed the land; the land knew nought of him,
Ugony's great-grandson, nor his story,
And yet to leave the land was to leave all
Except bare life: he would farewell Croftnie
And look to see him in the coming years.

A green rush that none reacheth,
A broom-blossom on the mountain,
A King's daughter. . . .

So Croftnie chanted, and young Lowry Maen
Saw the King's daughter who held up her hand
To gift the Harper; her face he saw:
Her eyes had light in them—
'Twas like the light of summer day beside
The feeble glow of springtime afternoon
That was the light in others of mankind,
And this light rested on her face and made it
Bright, as though a happiness were round it:
Else it was but a simple, youthful face.

[45]

She held herself as to the Harper's tune—
A green rush that none reacheth,
A broom-blossom on the mountain,
A King's daughter....
But stayed her gaze on the young man who came
To them up from the sea. He grew fearful
That he should lose his speech, again be "maen,"
But thought "Until she wishes well to me,
I cannot leave the land she walks upon."

He would not go upon the Gaulish ship,
He said, and said no more, and thereupon
The Harper made him known, and Seoriah
One and the other pressed to be his guests.

Then came the others: Sedna and Aleel
Together, and then Naale who strode up,
And in his cut speech told them that his fellow
Had gone; they would not have his company.
None knew where he had gone, nor did they name
His father when they spoke of Cavach's son.

A rough defile
That journeying upon was dangerous

Led into Seoriah's little kingdom; 'twas
The custom to make poems in praise of it,
And so avert the perils of the way.
And where a torrent like a white dog leaped
Across their path they stayed to make their poems.
They shouted them up to a rock that sent
The words back to them. All judged that Miria's,
That mentioned the eagle with wings of grey
That perched upon the rock and harshly screamed,
The best of all the praises they had made.

Seoriah and Miria on their horse,
The three young men who, turn about, gave place
To Croftnie on a horse, and Lowry Maen
Who kept up with the others though on foot,
Went on upon the journey. Never word
Was between Lowry Maen and Miria,
But yet their looks when he would pass by them,
Her and her father at whose back she was,
Showed each the other's longings.
                                    So they came
To Seoriah's dwelling.
                        It was twilight:
Cackling, the geese went by men on the lawn,

Geese from the lakeside coming, and the men
Cried out on King Seoriah, "What we've had
On this lawn was no judgment." They turned then
To Lowry Maen who in the twilight stood,
And said, "The woad belonging to the Queen
Was cropped and by our sheep, and here stay we
For judgment."

           Then, in a deep voice speaking,
As though a line of Kings spoke through his lips,
The young man whom they turned to answered them,
"The woad again will grow cropped by your sheep,
And the sheep's wool will grow; therefore, the fleece
Goes to the Queen to make up for her loss."
And the lank men upon the lawn cried out,
"A judgment, surely! thus a King's son speaks!"
"No King's son," said Seoriah, "and I said
'Tis not my day for judgments—come to-morrow,
And judging on this lawn I'll bear in mind
This young man's saying. Now we'll all go in."
And he took Sedna, Naale and Aleel
Into the house with Miria; his wife
Welcomed the Harper and his fosterling.

Fresh fire was piled; the boardings of red yew
Were smooth and polished, and there were on them
Rondures of copper that the fire lit.
The benches had upon them otter-skins,

The board was set up: there were placed on it
Green herbs and freshly gathered heath-berries,
Fine meal with honey mixed; methers filled
With sloe-juice and fermented honey mingled—
Mead of the land: Miria's was this service,
And when she laid a platter on the board
Or mether, more wonder was about her
Than when she stood beneath the oak, her head
Held backward by a bush of hair the sun
Glinted, or when she stood, her arms raised
Watching the eagle that flew close to her,
Through misty air to perch upon the rock.
So thought the youth who watched her, Lowry Maen,
His heart strained in him with the sense that she
Was there, and far away, and close beside him.
And then he whispered Croftnie, telling him
That when he had spoken with her he would go
Gather a band about him, and some time
Ways would be shown them to turn on Cavach—

Cavach, who had many now against him.
But he would have to tell all this to her.

Then when the Harper at the open door
Stood, to him went Miria—
Upon his cheeks her two hands she laid,
And Croftnie knew that she was suppliant to him—
For what he knew. He bent his head to her.

The goose that had been turning
Before the fire was placed upon the board,
And all but Lowry Maen and Miria
Had talk and answers that kept laughter up:
They stayed around the board
To break nut-clusters and share the kernels,
And then they went where firelight showed their
    faces,
Sitting on benches there.

It was custom
In Seoriah's house, after the feast was finished,
To make up staves of verse: this one or that
Would make up half a stave: another one
Would close the half-stave with two lines of verse.

Miria and her mother
Were good at this, but now Seoriah's daughter
Stayed silent, as though heavy were her thoughts.

But 'twas to her that Harper Croftnie
Offered a half-stave—this.—

"The Harper who has magic can make three
Tunes, passing others, sound upon his strings."

Miria, speaking slowly, closed the verse.—

"Laughter and Weeping are the tunes that he
Sounds, and another, Sleep the third string brings."

Croftnie another half-stave offered her.—

"Which is the tune that's wanted above all,
When he, the Harper who has magic, plays?"

Miria answered, and all praised the cunning
That found the words and sounds that answered his.—

"I would have Slumber, for if that befall
Laughter and Weeping are upon its ways."

[51]

Then Croftnie's fingers went upon the harp:
They made a sound like murmuring of leaves.
Miria to the open door went softly,
And Lowry Maen who could no longer stay
Removed from her, went to the open door.
Oh, Harper play
With all the magic that is yours! He played
And Seoriah and his wife and the three youths,
And the servants behind the leathern curtain
With heads were sunken, heard
The forest's murmur stealing on the sea's.

"Where do you come from? Whither do you go?
Will that black ship carry you from our land?"
She spoke to know how real he was, and he
Put hands upon her face to feel how real
Those cheeks, that brow were, and the throat,
And felt the lips that she had placed on his.
Then they went on as though they two had come
Out of a mist; happily they went; they heard
The calls of curlew and flying wild-geese,
And then they heard the foaming of the water
Making its famous fall—so far they'd gone!

"But if you go will you come here again?
You should not! What can we do to keep you
Here, and please you? What would you have of us?
My father is an honored King amongst
The Kings; we have been heard of; Cavach's son . . .
He has come here to gain me, that King's son."

Even as she spoke the name he knew that he
Had heard this fall of water and had seen
The stones beyond, that cromlech! He was Maen:
He knew his father had been slain by Cavach,
And knew that he must live till he brought powers
That would condemn one who had made blood pour
That must be still upon the grass down there.
And wild was he to think that any band
That he might gather could throw Cavach down—

[53]

Only the men from Gaul with iron weapons
Could make his downfall sure; the ship was there,
And presently that ship would sail for Gaul,
And terror and confusion would over-rule
The land because it sailed for Gaul without him.
"I will to Gaul," he cried, "I must to Gaul;
I will come back; I must come back to you."
She said no word but looked into his eyes.
"I will stay here and hide in caves," he said.
"I will hide with you." Their arms were round
Each other. They heard the water-fall
Making a sound that drowned all other sounds,
And then the fall
Of their hearts' blood that dumbed the water's fall.

Once more they moved, but now they moved so
　slowly
The deer stayed near them; Miria trembled
Because she would not be alone with him,
Nor with herself alone; because she was not
The same who went across her father's threshold.

They found awakening sleepers in the house.
Her mother stirred the fire to a blaze,

And in that blaze Miria stood and sighed.
Her mother said, "This is a woman's sigh,
On parting from the man who's had her love."
Her father said, "She had a maid's swift glance,
And now she has the slow look of a wife."

Naale flung on Lowry Maen; the two
Grappled. And then there was a din outside
Of baying dogs and barking dogs and men
Shouting. King Seoriah's watchman stood
Inside the door and cried out that the precinct
Was all encircled with King Cavach's men,
And that they'd break through even to the hearth:
They'd come to kill or drag a man away.

Miria said to Lowry Maen, "Away,
And I will live until you're here again."
And Seoriah said, "Away, and fast away!
I will forbid these youths to press on you."
And Croftnie said, "Make your way to the ship,
And in some years return; here I will stay
And here will stay the girl whom I'll guard."
Miria with pale lips said, "Do that—go."
Then Lowry Maen

Slipped from the door, and running for his life
Distanced the hounds that would have pulled him
    down,
And like an otter swam and 'scaped the hounds
And watching men, and travelled to the sea,
And when day came was underneath the oak.
There he mixed blood
With blood of those who would make him a brother,
And went upon the Gaulish ship and sailed
Before King Cavach's men came on the beach.

THE SIXTH PART

I know why I have better listeners here
Than I shall have when I speak at the Fair,
And tell this story from the sacred mound.
For of the stock of him who sheltered Croftnie
And his dumb charge when they came from the river,
Is he whose hearth I speak at these short nights.
My story waits: something handed down
Might give a glint to that which I must show—
Aye, House-master. . . .

My father used to tell . . .

My story waits. A listener now am I.

The seasons were not fair in Ireland then,
Nor could they be, since an unrightful King
Had rule; grain lessened, cattle pined,
And on the forest-ground there was less beech,
Less oak mast; less fish were in the streams;
And then as men grew desperate, wars grew up:
Folk did not know
When wars had ceased for they grew up again,
And every wattled house had its dissension,
And laws meant anything that ill-ruled men

Might say they meant, and all this bad grew worse
After Leary's son left Ugony's land.

Aye, so they tell. The like will I tell too.

Old houses then went down . . .

As a King who hears
A treasure-ship is wrecked upon his coast,
And calls a company, hurries to the shore,
All eager to endow himself with wreck
Of others' hopes, was Naale when he heard
That Seoriah's kingdom had been over-run
With spoilers, and that she who would have crowned
Their spoil had 'scaped them and was fugitive:
He took a hunter and a huntress
To search with him the crannies of the land.

She did not know, Miria,
That she was captive till they topped a ridge
And saw beyond the lake walls with no roof,
A house forsaken now that was her father's.
And then they had to bind her hands and feet
And carry her along: so she was brought
Into her suitor's and her captor's house.

He would do all things for her if she would,
As a King's daughter, plight herself to him.
For all his pleas, for all his angers did
To her, she would not; thrall to him was she,
And to the passion that had hold of him,
And she would be his thrall and nothing more.

Two moons went by. One evening as she stood
Beside the door, Miria heard a note
That was a harp-string struck, and knew that she
Was not forsaken. Then there came a day
When men ran here and there and women gathered
At watching-places, and hounds were cried on,
And Naale had a mind but on the chase.
She stole away, and like the wild-goat's kid,
Her spancel broken, making for the ledge,
Quickly, lightly, hurried from house and field.

A man was in a covert she was drawn to
By sounds, and he was Croftnie and he knew
A way to bring her to a hiding-place.

He sheared her hair, he stained her face, he gave
Another garment to her and they fled.
Her father's land they could not venture in,

And so they headed for another place.
But where they went the land was always turned
Inside out like a badger hung for meat.
They skirted lands where war was scraping out
What people kept as one scrapes out a pot,
And came to where was Croftnie's foster-father.

And there they bided in a nook unknown:
On Miria's cheek, the breadth of a man's hand,
A stain remained, and down along her neck.
And Croftnie who had stained her face and taken
Almost all away could not that mark clear,
That darkened patch upon fair cheek and neck.
She wore it as a man who held a fort
Whose fall's forgotten wears the arrow's gash.
She learned to knit the nets and helped to weave
The boats, and would not be forlorn—
She would not have a day find her forlorn.
She grew to have a beauty that was like
The beauty harp-strings tell of when they tell
Of women walking on the Ancient Plain.

They heard of Naale: how he was attacked
By Cavach's men, Conaing leading them,
And how he, fighting angrily, was killed.

And so the way was open for them back
To Seoriah's kingdom; in the evenings,
Croftnie and Miria, as they looked at
What happened on the stream or on the bank,
Wild-duck's, or water-hen's, or otter's doings,
Would speak of Lowry Maen and wonder much
What he was doing in that far-off place.

Beside another river Lowry Maen
Watched warriors and women,
Old men and children, cross in boats and rafts,
With horses, cattle, wagons of a tribe.
They had left their old fields, and had left the hills,
And river they had named to find new lands,
And Catumandus was there to order
Their movement and to give them their division—
Catumandus the over-king of Gaul
Whom Lowry Maen attended; the exile
Changed by all was shown to him said:
"These are what Kings should be—
These iron-using Kings; their wills are not
Strained through such speeches as old men must make
In long assemblies, nor hobbled like the horses
Outside the camp, by custom of the tribe.

[63]

They can pick out the deep-soiled lands to settle
On them the young men and the childing women;
They can have forests hewn down, and wolf-packs
Hunted to death; their will is done
By thrice ten thousand men; they can grow up
To the full height of Kings: I dreamt of such
When I was tongue-tied, wandering with Croftnie:
I dreamt that there were such, the Sons of Bran.
And now I know them and know one who'll aid me.
Cavach! The hundredth part of the armed men
That this King has would overthrow a King
That holds the kingship as my father might
Have held it; as King Ugony, because
The race was sacred and they'd stood upon
The Stone of Destiny that roared beneath them:
They have but props of custom to uphold them.
I can bring
Another image of a King to Ireland;
Make all the tribes know that a King is there;
Smite reivers on the coast and mould the tribes
Into a mighty tribe whose power will spread
Beyond the seas; I'll be the one who'll do it.
Croftnie would question, but he does not know
That Ugony's rule can never be again
Anywhere in these lands."

      Croftnie and Miria,
The ship from Gaul having come, went to the port,
And Croftnie waited for the merchant-chief,
And spoke to him about the youth who'd gone
Last year upon the ship—how had he fared?
He had been well received by Catumandus,
The merchant told him, was already noted,
And likely still to be beside the King.
Then Croftnie the Harper asked the merchant
To have a message brought to that young man,
Telling him that a King's daughter waited
For his return, and that her father's lands
Were open to attackers; there was only
An old man's wits to keep her safe for him.

A morning came when Catumandus chose
A leader for the band who were to guard
A tribe that he would settle in the south,
And Lowry Maen he chose. And on that day
When all was stirring for the march, the exile
Marked a man with shaggy hounds approach,
And knew these hounds had sprung through forest-
    glades
In Ireland: from him he heard
How an old man who played upon a harp
Had spoken to the master of the ship
Asking him to let Lowry Maen, a captain,
Know that a King's daughter waited for him,
Who had not now the safe days of before,
Who had, indeed, been captive and was rescued.
Her father's lands were open to attackers:
There was only
An old man's wits to keep her safe for him.

The beauty of Miria
Came over him: he saw her happy face,
Lighted and changing like a dancing leaf;
Then with resolve and sorrow in the eyes
That bade him go and told him to return,

[66]

And the flushed face he held between his hands—
Miria—who was there to guard her now
That Cavach's men had broken through the bound
Of Seoriah's kingdom? Lowry Maen's heart shook
With heavy groans. Wagons were creaking now,
And herds were moving, and his men were mounted,
And he must lead them; he would give his will,
His mind to them, lead them, and lead also
His heart from its forebodings: he would give
His will, his mind, to Catumandus's purpose,
Accomplish his design and gain his favor
To use the iron mass against King Cavach:
Thereafter would be peace—peace for Miria,
For him and for his land—soon it would be!
All was laid out before him like red iron
That he would strike and shape without delay.

THE SEVENTH PART

An old man with a cloak of grey about him
Welcomed them from the low door of a hut:
He was King Seoriah; his wife was dead
And buried, and his mind was at a loss.

Miria and the Harper, home again,
Surveyed the losses; as they did they saw
The losses lessen; things had passed their worst.
Raiders no more came over that rough border,
And Seoriah's folk had certain stores of grain:
They took the sheep and cattle out of caves,
And with their King to stand as head to them,
And Croftnie and Miria counselling,
They came to be a hopeful folk once more,
Men of the spade, sickle and pasture-field,
And the assembling-place.

[71]

This in a year:
Then the ship came from Gaul and they had word
Of Lowry Maen: the youth had gone afar,
But would be back in Catumandus's camp
By the next time the ship went back to Gaul.
When Croftnie brought these tidings to Miria,
She would have pined but that her father said,
"Get you a husband—
'Tis time indeed—I should have a grandson."
"I'll take a husband,"
She told him, "when our house is built again."
She got her father thinking of the house
With all its planks and beams and doors and thatch,
And had eight craftsmen with their wives to come
Where stand of timber was, and had the one
Who had the name of Gobaun Saor begin
The cutting and the trimming of the timber.

The work went on, and when there came a day
When all that could be used of the old house
Was gathered in one place and could be looked on,
Miria walked alone by the lake-shore.
She thought herself unfriended; the water
Was lapping on the stones; a bird she heard:

No other bird upon the lake nor on
The shore gave answer, and the cry went on
As if the bird, knowing no answer could be,
Told itself all its loss and all day told it.
And Miria who was full of care that day,
And loneliness, made a plaint had in it
The bird's cry and the lapping on the stones.

She sang the plaint to Croftnie; then he played
Chords of the tune that he would never play—
The Sorrow Tune: he told her he would play
Those chords and chant the plaint unto the one
She waited for.

       And when the ship had come
He went down to it and with rings of gold
Paid for his passage; they brought the Harper
Where they had brought his fosterling before.
Now going on the land Croftnie beheld
Sights that made him know how separate
This land was from his own and Lowry Maen's:
Saw smiths hammering upon blazing
Iron lumps; warriors with shaven
Faces, and round shields with iron swords

[73]

That were in wooden sheaths hung on their belts:
Even their horses' hoofs were iron-shod:
The valleys and the hills of Ireland
Were far away when he looked on such gear.

And they could answer him, these iron men,
With words that were less strange as they talked on;
They had familiar voices and a way
Of holding their heads up and laughing gaily,
And when he heard their singing he could think
They'd come no further than three fields away
From Leary's house; yet they were men who'd
     marched
As far as to the City of the Greeks,
Or further south, the City of the Ships
Where Argonthonios reigned, the Silver King.

Croftnie was brought into the assembly,
And spoke and told the chieftains of the Gauls
How they had come from the one stock, their race
And his: in Murias or Falias,
In Findrias or Gorias they were one,
And that was when the stars men name The Seven
Were seven indeed—not six as now they are,

And their folk took to wagons and were here,
With bright lands open to them, and his folk
Took ships and went out on the ocean-ways
And reached an island with a sacred name.

Then, in his chariot, Catumandus
Watching his soldiers marching back again,
Croftnie saw; he stayed beside the chariot:
He saw the dust before them, and he saw
The files and files of iron-armed men,
And with the troopers and among the chiefs
He saw the one whom he had come to seek.
Then when the army settled in the camp,
And mules and horses stood beside the outposts
Swinging their tails against the swarms of flies,
One had the Harper brought into his tent.
Bronzed was Lowry Maen
And with a quick, commanding look: he heard
How Seoriah's lands were ravaged, and his house
Destroyed; how Miria was made captive
And kept the thrall of Naale who'd been killed,
And how they lived in Seoriah's kingdom now
Like men whose fortress is upon a cliff.

He heard all told
About Miria, and he said no word;
Then asked of Cavach: where now was the King?
And saying that, since warfare now was rife
Throughout the land, Cavach must have fighters,
And that his son who had resource enough,
Could lead a host of men, he stayed in silence
As one who plans.

       Then Harper Croftnie knew
That Lowry Maen, his fosterling, had memories
Forbye the memories of Miria's love,
Or days beside the river; he had memories
Of conquests; when he'd go to Ugony's land
It would be as a soldier venturing on
Another conquest: so the Harper thought
As Lowry Maen, his hands upon his knees,
Sat silent.

       Then Croftnie his harp lifted
To his shoulder, and played the Sorrow Tune—
The first chords only, and as he played them,
In the young captain the spirit changed.
All he had lost was present and still lost:
His father who would have him sit to hear
The story-teller by the fitful fire,
Aye, and his uncle
Who had murdered, was King, and yet had been
A man who wept to see a broken horse,
And Croftnie whose years had withered away
Giving him care—dead, doomed and old were they;
And they were gone, the evenings when men came
Up from the river with the shining fish,

And the water-hen went on her lonely way.
Croftnie, the tune playing more lightly now,
Sang Miria's song; her sorrow deepened his:
Lonely she was, and what had he to do
But end that loneliness and rest her head
Upon his breast—what else was there to do
Where Life was always running after Death?

"Why are we in this land?" he said to Croftnie,
"Our memories are not here," and he rose up
And went into the assembly of the Gauls
Where Catumandus sat, and asked a levy
Of Gaulish soldiers to be led by him,
And brought across the sea to help him win
His father's kingdom. And because the tribe
That had moved to the south had been secured
By Lowry Maen's device, and soldiers were
Too many in the camp of Catumandus,
Three thousand men were granted Lowry Maen,
Armed with iron swords and long blue lances,
And thirty ships to take them would be loaned him
For payment in the gold of Ireland,
And Lowry Maen should settle on good lands
His Gaulish aids and should find wives for them,

And with the soldiers there would also go
Smiths who would work the iron of the land.

　　So thirty ships,
A hundred men in each, set sail from Gaul,
And Lowry Maen was captain; Croftnie
Sailed back with them but had no word to say.

The tale is old: Dinn Righ is fallen in
That had its name from men of Gaulish speech,
And in our warrior's hands are now the swords
Patterned on those that once were foreigners'.

O Story-teller, tell of triumph gained.

That will I at the fair where Tighernmas
Is honored, and where Lowry Loingsech,
Once Lowry Maen, Ugony's great-grandson,
Has games that keep his name in memory.

What is a story without triumph gained?

The blue lances and long-reaching swords
Prevailed against the bronze—it was to be:

You who have lived with parting and with death
Need not hear now about the reddened spears,
Need not hear now about defenders slain,
Need not hear now about the roofs in flame.
Now is a horse being shod with shoes of iron,
A burning and a piercing and a weight
Being put on hoofs that had left hardly track
On plain and hillside: now the first one foaled
In Ireland has iron on his hoofs,
And a King mounts him, Ugony's great-grandson,
And Leary's son, and on and on he hies,
And gallops up a rough defile and comes
Where stands a ruler's house.
                                        'Tis open wide:
Inside a fire is burning on the stones,
And lighting up the boards of polished yew,
And copper circlets. He has come within.
Who is it weeps? Miria, for his presence
Shakes tears from her, as from the chestnut blossom
The long-kept rain-drops fall in sudden wind.

Weeping, she's held by him. " 'Tis over now,"
She said, and to the board went and there took
The cup of water was her pledge to him,

And held herself upright, her wide eyes on him,
And he half-drained the cup and gave it back,
And she drank what was left, and their lips met.

And they were talking, held to one another
Of things were done, and things that would be done,
And in the gloom there was an old man moving,
One with a coat of woven goats' hair on him,
And muttering, " 'Tis time I had a grandson,"
And Miria, for whom such words had been
So dismal, laughed, and loud laughed Lowry Maen,
Now Lowry Loingsech, Lowry the Mariner,
Who with his arm around Miria came
Into the firelight; then Seoriah
Knew him and cried out, "The mountainy men
Said a king's son without doubt you were."
"I am your daughter's husband, and the King
In Cavach's place," said Lowry Loingsech.
"My feet were on the Stone
Of Destiny; 'twas heard to roar beneath
With sound of the four seas of Ireland,
And with us two are nighted by your hearth
Another line, another rule begins."

[81]

Macmillan 1-20-38